Dual Role Ministry

First Choice or Mixed Blessing?

Nigel Peyton

Ministry Development Adviser and
Priest-in-Charge, Lambley, Diocese of Southwell

GROVE BOOKS LIMITED
RIDLEY HALL RD CAMBRIDGE CB3 9HU

Contents

Acknowledgements
I am indebted to Ian Bunting, Rosemary Gatie, Pauline Hutchinson, Andy Knowles, Gordon Oliver, Sue Parsons, Anne Peyton, David Tilley, Rod Allon-Smith, Tony Tucker and Ruth Yeoman for help with this booklet.

The Cover Illustration is by *Design*works Clipart

First Impression March 1998
ISSN 0144-171X
ISBN 1 85174 368 5

1
Introduction

Scarcely six months after the Labour Party's landslide victory at the 1997 General Election, Prime Minister Tony Blair faced a serious parliamentary backbench revolt against proposals to cut welfare benefits for lone parents. Shortly afterwards he received deputations from coal miners and disabled people who were fearful about their future. The large number of Labour MPs who voted against their Government were reminding the modernizing zealots of New Labour that traditional socialist values concerning the poor and vulnerable were still around. Almost everyone agrees that the Welfare State needs reforming—the arguments are about how best to achieve a just and affordable system of social support for the needy. New Labour cannot entirely lose its Old Labour shadow as it seeks to modernize. Organizations which rise to the challenge of change ignore their roots and past at their peril. Somehow the new vision has to connect or at least coexist with what people say has 'always been the way we do things here.'

The churches face a similar dilemma: how to become 'New Church' while traditional ways of doing things are very much the norm. In particular, the Church of England is struggling to rediscover itself as a national church in a post-Christendom Britain characterized by decline in churchgoing and 'believing without belonging.' The insights of sociologists of religion have helped us better to understand this crucial transition. In particular the work of Robin Gill and Grace Davie deserves close attention by church communities as they look to a future beyond decline.[1] Commenting on the latest religious trends, Davie observes the significant mismatch between widespread nominal affiliation to the churches and a small and reducing constituency of committed Christians. 'Clearly it was different in the past and may well be so in the future; in the meantime this is the context in which the churches are obliged to operate in the late 1990s…the combination of belief without belonging offers some advantages and some disadvantages to the institutional churches. Working out the implication of such patterns for pastoral practice should be high on their collective agendas.'[2]

Treasure New and Old

The biblical image which may help us here is that of the householder's treasure, new and old, to which Jesus drew his disciples' attention: 'Therefore every scribe who has been trained for the kingdom of heaven is like the master of a household who brings out of his treasure what is new and what is old'

---

1   Robin Gill, *Beyond Decline* (London: SCM, 1988) and *The Myth of the Empty Church* (London: SPCK, 1993); Grace Davie, *Religion in Britain since 1945* (Oxford: Blackwell, 1994).
2   Grace Davie in Peter Brierley (ed), *UK Christian Handbook Religious Trends No 1* (London: Christian Research, 1997) p 0.3.

(Matt 13.51–52 NRSV). Coming at the conclusion of Matthew's significant collection of 'parables about the kingdom' in chapter thirteen, we realize its gospel message: that harnessing the best of our resources, whether tried and tested or brand new, determines the quality of our response to God's challenge to participate wholeheartedly in his purposes. Matthew's view of continuity between the God of Israel, the Lord Jesus of the Church, and the Ruler at the end of time encourages us to expect that God is revealed anew in every age in his church and its ministries.[3]

The growing realization over a number of years that we are in a new and difficult situation has led the Church to explore fresh patterns of ministry and to reassess clergy roles, just as in the wider social context the roles of doctors, teachers and other professional groups are being questioned and changed. A particular focus for change is the reducing numbers of full-time stipendiary clergy and the increased lay involvement in the life of the Church. Accompanying these developments has been a literature about 'new ministry' whose shifting focus documents the passage of change. For example, twenty years ago we looked at the careers of the clergy,[4] then the Tiller Report challenged us with new ideas about ministerial organization[5] and we were also reminded that all Christians are called to ministry.[6] Anthony Russell described the historical emergence of the clergyperson as an incomplete professional role[7] while Christopher Moody in a fascinating book entitled *Eccentric Ministry* questioned that professionalism.[8] More recently Robin Greenwood recast the public representative minister's presiding role within a theology of mission and ministry rooted in a contemporary trinitarian theology of relationships in the church[9] while Ian Bunting has proposed the 'pathfinder-leader' role as a suitable model of ministry today.[10] In the literature we observe a shift from interest in the professional identity of clergy to a wider concern about the personal vulnerability within Christian ministry, and the expectations and experiences of ministers.

The transition in ideas about ministry is not peculiar to Anglicans. However, as we approach the millennium, the pressure is on the Church of England's clergy deployment strategy, caused by increased retirements, an uncertain number of vocations, and a far greater financial responsibility laid upon the local church

3 J C Fenton, *St Matthew* (London: SCM, 1963) pp 128, 230f. J D Kingsbury, *The Parables of Jesus in Matthew 13* (London: SPCK, 1969) pp 17–21, 125–129.
4 Robert Towler and A P M Coxon, *The Fate of the Anglican Clergy* (London: Macmillan, 1979). Neil Burgess, 'Clergy Careers in the Church of England this Century' in *Crucible* (London: Board of Social Responsibility, July 1995) pp 127–136.
5 John Tiller, *A Strategy for the Church's Ministry* (London: CIO Publishing, 1983).
6 General Synod Board of Education, *All Are Called—Towards a Theology of the Laity* (London: CIO Publishing, 1985).
7 Anthony Russell, *The Clerical Profession* (London: SPCK, 1980) p 239.
8 Christopher Moody, *Eccentric Ministry* (London: Darton, Longman & Todd, 1992) pp 52, 58.
9 Robin Greenwood, *Transforming Priesthood* (London: SPCK, 1994) pp 141–179.
10 Ian Bunting, *Models of Ministry* (Grove Pastoral Series No 54, Cambridge: Grove Books, 1993) pp 4, 22–24.

rather than reliance upon central subsidy.[11] The advent of non-stipendiary ministries has only partially met the need for clergy and it has become evident that
dioceses wish to take more control of the recruitment and selection, training and
deployment of their clergy. Hence the noticeable expansion in recent years of
Local Non Stipendiary Ministry Schemes and experimental ways of using retired
clergy, Readers and other authorised laity to be the 'parson person' in the local
community, often in local ministry teams.[12] What emerges is a mixed economy of
ministry in which lay and ordained ministers are called to work in creative partnerships beyond parochial structures, away from the constraints of the intramural church. They are now called into the newer communities of common concern,
and into radical ways of becoming 'church for the unchurched' and being faithful
Christians in the world of daily living. The discovery of the appropriate role for
the full-time stipendiary minister in all this change is an urgent task for the Church,
as is the need for training and support for laity and clergy to do things differently.

In realizing that the inherited paradigms of parish, priest and church are now
less plausible servants of the Church's mission and ministry, another response (as
in the Labour Party) is to modernize the infrastructure.[13] There is a concern to
bring closer together policy-making and resourcing, theology and practice, and
to streamline decision-making. Reactions are symptomatic of the New Church
dilemma, the clash between necessary change and 'the way we do things here.'
Tony Berry, a member of General Synod, warns that working for change in the
church community is complex and uncertain: 'it is not possible to address the
underlying assumptions for they have become undiscussable. The major issue it
appears is the anxiety created by the pressures upon the church and its decline.
The defences that are being erected to contain these anxieties are not discussable
as indeed are the anxieties. This undiscussability may itself be undiscussable.'[14]

Dual Role Ministry

Dual Role Ministry (DRM) is a particular response by Anglicans and other
churches to changed times. In essence it means deploying a stipendiary minister
to two, usually rather different sorts of ministry, often with contrasting expectations. Dual Role Ministers (DRMs) are frequently required to cross boundaries,
change roles and employ various skills. DRM illustrates all too clearly the pathol-

---

11 In 'Stipendiary Clergy: Supply and Demand 1996–2001,' a consultative exercise with dioceses
   by the Advisory Board of Ministry, it was revealed that dioceses are expecting to deploy 6.2%
   more clergy than are expected to be available in 2001. In *Recovering Confidence, The Call to
   Ordained Ministry in a Changing World* (London: ABM, 1996) p 24 the need for a culture of
   vocation and recruitment was highlighted.
12 A review of LNSM schemes *Strangers in the Wings* is due to be published by the Advisory
   Board of Ministry in 1998. Examples of fresh ministry patterns may be found in Nigel Peyton
   (ed), *Ministry Stories* (Southwell: Diocese of Southwell Ministry Group, 1996).
13 The Report of the Archbishops' Commission on the Organization of the Church of England,
   Working as One Body (London: Church House Publishing, 1995); the Report of the review
   group appointed by the Standing Committee of the General Synod, *Synodical Government in
   the Church of England: A Review* (London: Church House Publishing, 1997).
14 Anthony J Berry, 'Control in a Social Institution, A Case Study: the Church of England,' a
   paper given at the Annual Conference of the British Academy of Management 1996.

ogy of a church in decline and the pressures of modern ministry. Bishop Bill Ind once remarked that DRMs are 'at the sharp end of the search for the right strategy for a Church serving the whole nation' and need 'to be jobbing theologians, holding together the edges of the Church, catholic and local.'[15] This is a tall order! Hence our questioning subtitle, 'First choice or mixed blessing?' Many of us in DRM experience both these possibilities, and this booklet explores the reasons why: firstly by looking at the growth and rationale for DRM; then secondly, by examining the making and sustaining of dual role appointments; and thirdly, by reflecting theologically on the value of dual role as a model of ministry, and on role complexity in contemporary ministry. While it is hoped that this might become a useful 'Handbook for Dual Role Ministry,' filling a gap in the literature, it remains a modest beginning, raising questions that will require more systematic attention by dioceses, the Advisory Board of Ministry and others at a later date. In many respects DRM opens an important window onto an uncertain future, and into our understanding of the ministries undertaken by all God's people in Christ's name. This booklet may provide some encouragement to those with a care or responsibility for ministry in the churches.

Perhaps the biggest challenge for clergy nowadays, especially the full-time stipendiary clergy, is to work with old and new expectations and methods at the same time within their communities. For example, some Anglicans mourn the loss of 'common worship'—replaced by a more *á la carte* menu where the old and the new are kept separate, equally valid and valued. Yet the postmodern paradigms are precisely those of individualism and consumer choice—TV channels and the supermarket. Grace Davie suggests that even belief itself is fragmenting, 'No longer anchored by the regular repetition of liturgy or by the half-remembered Bible stories from Sunday school, belief mutates. The concept of God becomes increasingly subjective: individuals simply pick and mix from the variety on offer.'[16] Variety is the spice of life for DRMs, bringing out treasure old and new in ministry. It is not unusual for DRMs to combine traditional and radical approaches in their work, moving from one to the other on a daily basis. In the following section we shall take a closer look at the character and scope of DRM.

---

15 Bill Ind from his keynote address at the annual Dual Role Ministry Consultation at Launde Abbey, March 1995, reported in *Twofold*, the newsletter of the National Network for Dual Role Ministry, Autumn 1995.

16 Grace Davie, *UK Christian Handbook Religious Trends No 1, op cit*, p 0.4.

2

The Advent of Dual Role Ministries

Two for the Price of One

What is particular about *Dual Role Ministry*? Surely busy ministers perform many different roles on a daily basis? While this is, of course, true, what seems to have happened in recent years is a more deliberate deployment of clergy in the Church of England and partner churches who 'do more than one job.' On this basis the Church is implicitly expecting two ministries for the price of one. It is a model of pastoral organization which until recently has not always been recognized as such.[17] However, the growing numbers of such dual role ministers (DRMs) have gradually developed a professional self-consciousness, sharing common concerns and good practice through a national network and an annual residential consultation. It would be a real help if the Church Commissioners' clergy database could distinguish DRMs on the computerized national payroll. At present there is a confusion between true DRM and other categories, for example, married clergy couples sharing ministries or clergy holding benefices in plurality. There is no dedicated category in the programme which can give accurate information about the spread of DRM, although this point has been raised at Church House.

Portraits of Dual Role Ministers

So what does DRM look like? A working definition is, *'dual role ministry describes posts which formally combine two sorts of ministerial work, frequently with divergent foci of responsibility and accountability.'* The Anglican bishop or his equivalent licenses the minister into dual roles, usually on a time-limited contract, and resignation has to be from both posts, unlike, for example, the office of rural dean. Unlike the parochial clergy in their varied roles, DRMs cannot choose to neglect either part of their fundamental role division. Three portraits of dual role ministers will serve to illustrate what DRM looks like.

Tony is Priest-in-Charge of a united benefice comprising four rural parishes (total population 1,100) combining this with an advisory role as Diocesan Officer for Tourism. His appointment in 1996 provided him with a job description for two days each week—liaising with local authorities and their tourism officers across the county, and relating to parishes as an adviser and a resource. Tony has formed a Churches Tourism Resource Group and has national and ecumenical support but feels two days a week is insufficient time to do justice to the many possibilities. His advisory role is often that of 'broker' and he recognizes the need for public relations and training skills in this area. Tony's parish predecessor was

---

17 For example, DRM is omitted from the models of pastoral organization listed in Appendix 1 of David Parrot and David Field's, *Situation Vacant: A Guide to the Appointment Process in the Church of England* (Grove Pastoral Series No 65, Cambridge: Grove Books, 1996) p 24.

full time so four communities and congregations have needed time to adjust and to understand the new pastoral arrangements. There remains an expectation that the part-time vicar will manage to do all that his full-time predecessor did. Tony feels the pressure of multiple service-taking in rural communities. An open meeting is planned where, with the help of a consultant, parishioners will prioritize objectives and 'who does what.' Tony feels largely on his own in both jobs and recognizes the danger of isolation. Administratively, both roles are based in his vicarage and juggling work with his family and time off is tricky. Despite the problems, Tony 'loves the dynamic' of DRM: 'having other responsibilities releases different bits of me.'

Pauline, since 1995, has combined being Team Vicar in a large urban team ministry with chaplaincy at the town's hospital for 4 sessions (=14 hours) each week. Her brief from the NHS Trust was to establish a chaplaincy department in a new hospital which was replacing older premises on two sites. Pauline has successfully guided this development through many upheavals to a point where she has established a proper chapel and office together with two dozen trained voluntary hospital visitors. She has particularly enjoyed working with ecumenical colleagues over the years. Her parish district has a population of 5,000 and a church/community centre serving the poorer end of town. Pauline's predecessor was full time but the congregation supports her chaplaincy role and they are anxious that Pauline might have too much to do. Pauline does not have a job description, but honours a basic time-split between parochial ministry and chaplaincy sessions at the hospital, mostly on Mondays, Thursdays and Sundays. The two jobs cannot be too rigidly divided because the pastoral nature and unpredictability of both make boundaries less clear. Belonging to a congenial team ministry has made a lot of difference to Pauline, providing resources, policies, fellowship and support in times of real pressure—all of which counter clerical isolation. Her frustrations are about the expectations dual roles bring and the reality that each could be full time. However, Pauline realizes, 'I have to work with priorities, while keeping my sanity…sometimes I have to sit light to it and just go off and walk the dogs.'

Ian is a senior figure in the diocese who, since 1996, has combined the roles of Diocesan Director of Ordinands and Bishop's Research Officer. For some years previously he combined the DDO role with that of Urban Officer, living and assisting in an inner city parish. He moved location to the Bishop's Office because his two roles are both episcopally focused and cohere reasonably well in one place. The two job descriptions are not easy to timetable but, broadly, Ian deals with bishop's business in the mornings and sees potential ordinands in the afternoons. There is weekday pressure, assisting the bishop in the many demands made upon him, but he feels in control of his workload and able to prioritize. Ian takes Friday off and there is less pressure at the weekends. In the 1970s when Ian combined a traditional role as Director of Pastoral Studies at a theological college, with a pioneering one as Director of Studies of a new regional ordination course he experienced conflicts of time and accountability. Ian believes that DRM posts should be approached with caution because most people do not find it very easy to balance both parts of the job, and give themselves primarily to one or the other. Those who consider DRM should be aware that it is a very different form of diversity in ministry from that of the busy incumbent who acquires many additional involvements but who remains focused on the single-agenda primary role as incumbent.

The Growth of Dual Role Ministries

The above examples indicate the main kinds of ministerial roles likely to feature in dual role combinations: parish(es), chaplaincy(ies), sector(s) and diocesan advisory responsibility(ies). Since the pioneering description of DRM written by Tony Sparham in 1992[18] the number and diversity of dual role appointments has increased significantly. Research undertaken in 1995[19] and again more recently suggests that ten per cent of stipendiary Anglican clergy are in dual role.[20] That is approximately a thousand clergy of whom the national network is in touch with some twenty-five per cent. The research was conducted by careful monitoring of 1,427 appointments announced in the Gazette section of the *Church Times* over a nine-month period.

When we examine the 122 partnerships it becomes clearer what a diverse and considerable constituency DRM is. The combinations which dioceses sometimes conjure up are nothing if not imaginative! Three broad groups may be identified: parish plus chaplaincy posts (29.5%), parish plus diocesan advisory posts (46.7%) and miscellaneous combined posts (23.8%).

1. Taking both research samples together, *parish plus chaplaincy posts* (36) covered the following areas of ministry, where the style of chaplaincy will vary from traditional to quite innovative according to local circumstances:

   Schools, colleges, universities, hospitals, prisons, the police, industry, the communities of deaf or blind people, and those in the community with mental health difficulties or learning disabilities.

2. There were a substantial number of *parish plus diocesan advisory posts* (57). The sheer variety illustrates the contemporary repertoire of sector concerns which are so often now covered by dual role ministers:

   Spirituality, mission and evangelism, ecumenism and inter-faith work, religious education and church schools, children's and youth work, vocations and ordinands, clergy training (Post Ordination Training/Continuing Ministerial Education), women in ministry, Faith in the City/urban issues,

18 Tony Sparham 'Dual Role Ministries' *Expository Times*, Vol 103 No 5, February 1992.
19 Nigel Peyton 'Dual Role Ministries—Two for the price of one?' *Ministry: The Journal of The Edward King Institute for Ministry Development* No 27 Winter 1996.
20 Nigel Peyton 'Ten per cent DRM' *Twofold* the newsletter of the National Network for Dual Role Ministry Summer 1997.

rural affairs, adult education and lay training, Readers, Local and Non Stipendiary Ministry, race relations and Black Anglican concerns, stewardship, press and communications and Bishop's research.

3 The *miscellaneous posts* (29) included the following combinations:

Parish and overseas commissary, mission project leader and Adviser for Evangelism, Warden of Readers and co-ordinator of lay training and local ministry, Director of Ordinands and Bishop's Research Officer, Archbishop's Chaplain and Diocesan Missioner, university chaplain and ministry adviser, parish and bishop's assistant, parish and pastoral care of the clergy and their families. Residentiary Canons often combined cathedral duties with senior diocesan roles—as Directors of Ministry, Ordinands, Clergy Training or Mission, one was a diocesan secretary, another was an Adviser for the Paranormal. Two archdeacons ran parishes as did one assistant bishop. Two clergy combined a parish with being the diocesan retreat/conference centre warden. A theological college lecturer also ran a parish, another worked in communications. Two Bishops' Selection Secretaries were also appointed to advisory roles at the Advisory Board of Ministry.

In the research samples 7.8% of the appointments were as Rural/Area deans—are they also dual role ministers? As we have noted, the usual definition of DRM excludes them. Nevertheless many deans do share characteristics associated with dual role ministers, for example, wider responsibilities, different lines of accountability and the need for a significant time-share with his/her parish.[21] So also do parochial clergy who acquire additional 'portfolios.'

A Rationale for Dual Roles

The short answer to questions concerning the rationale for dual role ministry is expediency and choice. DRM appointments are a means of maintaining both parochial and sector ministry at a time of diminishing resources. Because the parochial pastoral model remains very powerful in the established church and because sector posts have to run the gauntlet of justification in any diocesan budget, bringing the two together seems the obvious solution. But as Michael Hill warns, 'DRMs are probably the product of a reactive management style—initially a shortage of money, now a clergy supply problem—how can we cover the same ground with fewer clergy? That means that DRMs have come on the scene without there being much thought about the impact on the individuals concerned or the wider Church.'[22] The temptation is to believe uncritically that a virtue can be made of 'two for the price of one.' Cuts in staffing budgets can thus be reinterpreted as a

---

21 Simon Brown, *The Role of Rural Deans* (Blandford Forum: Parish and People, 1994).
22 Michael Hill, speaking as an archdeacon and member of bishop's staff, from his keynote address at the annual Dual Role Ministry Consultation at Launde Abbey, April 1997. Reported more fully in *Twofold, op cit.*

diocesan policy to root advisers in parishes. Obviously, DRM posts can be chosen to spread diocesan sector ministry and advisory expertise around the deaneries, linked to ministry in the local church, often in the countryside but also in urban areas. They can provide ministry for the intramural church together with engagement with the world. There appears to be no shortage of takers amongst the clergy. Many are very excited by the prospect of DRM, while others are willing to give it a try. But there is nothing inevitable about a dual role post being first choice or first class. It would be interesting to know which of the forty-four dual role posts vacated in the research samples were continued as dual role appointments, and indeed to interview those who have left DRM about their experiences.

The remaining sections of this booklet will examine the advantages and problems of DRM. On the one hand, the combination of parochial and sector ministry can be stimulating. The minister is grounded in a base Christian community, yet with a portfolio beyond it—local and apostolic ministry feed each other. On the other hand, however, dual role appointments clearly bring their own particular pressures and these can intensify the normal trials which present day stipendiary clergy endure. Much depends on the personality and skills of the minister and the nature of the ministries being brought together. What the research figures do not tell us is just how carefully each dual role ministry has been thought out.

3
Making Dual Role Appointments

Partners Together

In 1994 three DRMs put together a paper entitled *Guidelines for Dual Role Ministries.*[23] A key concern of the authors was the need for careful preparations for dual role appointments and the sustaining of them thereafter. Experience indicated that the way different ministry roles were partnered required great care, and that the way in which dual role appointments were set up affected (for good or ill) early and formative expectations of the parties involved. There are four principle stakeholders in the establishment of a dual role ministry: a parochial ministry; a sector ministry; bishop's staff; and the prospective minister. It is important that their concerns come together in a job description which addresses the right questions. Allowing sufficient preparation time prior to any appointment to discuss proposals with the various parties involved and to write a job description is time well invested, which avoids misunderstandings or breakdown at a later stage. The costs of *ad hoc* decisions are borne personally by the postholder and sadly some DRMs have felt abused by the unreasonableness of the post created for them. This raises wider ethical questions about human resource management in the Church. The pressure for clergy to offer imaginative and flexible ministry nowadays equally challenges the Church to be a better employer, to take responsibility for a just and caring approach to personnel matters.[24] The few lay DRMs employed by the Church, for example in children's work, may have concerns in this area.

Bishop's Staff

Bishops and their staff have a key role in establishing a 'first choice' dual role appointment. It is at the staff meeting that the possibility of a dual role ministry will first be considered, often when a half-time sector role is proposed. Finding the right parish partner should reflect strategic planning rather than financial pragmatism.[25] Of course, personalia, availability, size and location can dominate the decision, but it should be questioned, for example, whether 'any rural base' will do. Similarly, in order not to compound competing priorities for the DRM, it is best to avoid linking a sector role to a parochial or other post that is itself already fragmented, or where local lay leadership is particularly weak. Special care should be taken where the minister will be new to the diocese, and/or 'in charge' in a parish for the first time, and/or where the sector role is a pioneering one.

23 Jeff Hopewell, Hazel Hughes and David Tilley, whose formative work is acknowledged and undergirds this Grove booklet.
24 *Ministry: A Pastoral Letter from the House of Bishops* (1994).
25 Robin Gill and Derek Burke, *Strategic Church Leadership* (London: SPCK, 1996) pp 37–49.

There is little point in setting ministers up for an impossible degree of newness and difficulty. Ideally at the licensing service the bishop ought to be confident in explaining the changed ministerial provision, the dual nature of the appointment, and in encouraging publicly all those who can contribute to its success. Thereafter it is crucial that bishop's staff do not forget about the post and postholder, making sure that support and review are available. Many DRMs approach their ministry with a high degree of energy, commitment and idealism. But the very positives of their character and ability can be their undoing, leading them to attempt too much. Some DRMs worry about performance and job security as freehold is replaced by limited contracts. Bishop's staff should be alert to these matters; it may help to consult the diocesan officer with most experience of DRM, and to follow a simple ten-step checklist:[26]

1. What are the needs for/expectation of the part-time sector .... role?
   Has the role been discussed and agreed by the diocesan group/board/council/committee to which the person appointed will relate?

2. What are the needs for/expectation of the part time parochial .... role?
   Has the proposed parish been consulted, and to what extent is it willing to develop its ministry with a dual role minister?

3. Who is preparing a draft job description and what needs to be written in?
   Consultation with both the sector and parochial foci will need to take place.
   * Is this the right partnership? If not or doubtful, delay or start afresh!

4. What qualities and skills are we seeking in the eventual postholder of this dual role ministry?

5. Who is suitable and available—in the diocese, elsewhere?
   Should we advertise?

6. Who should be shortlisted and interviewed?
   How are both sector and parish to be involved in this process?

7. Can we make a satisfactory appointment?
   * Is this the right person? If not or doubtful, delay [or consider (9) below]

8. What arrangements are necessary for the licensing service which will reflect both roles to be undertaken? Consult with sector and parish. Brief the licensing bishop.

---

26 Nigel Peyton, paper prepared for the Archbishops' Adviser for Bishops' Ministry, (1995).

9. What induction and early training needs does the prospective appointee have, and how can we ensure they are met? Refer these to appropriate diocesan (or outside) personnel.

10. What are the provisions for support and review? Again, refer these to appropriate personnel, setting a date for the review of the job description and progress during the first year.

The Parish Ministry

A parish should know as early as possible that a dual role appointment is being considered, particularly if the parish has enjoyed full-time stipendiary ministry hitherto or where DRM will be a completely new pattern for people. It is almost impossible to over-prepare! The meetings with bishop's staff which take place during the vacancy procedures under the Pastoral Measure are important in bringing out early resentments and expectations. However, in assenting to the inevitable, Parochial Church Councils need time to digest the proposals and the implications for them of having a 'DRM Vicar,' so an opportunity for informal consultations with those who have experienced DRM elsewhere can be valuable. For Anglicans the rural dean can support parishes in this position. It will be necessary to return to these topics after the DRM has begun as a normal periodic review of 'how things are going here.' Parishes which have thought about their community and priorities for mission (perhaps in a mission audit exercise) and which have adopted these in a parish development plan will know better how to use the resource of a dual role minister.[27] The Parish Statement prepared during a vacancy may not, however, reflect such sophistication, and frequently more thought will have been given to specifying the sector role which means that the parish-postholder relationship begins at a disadvantage.

The Sector Ministry

Discernment, again, is the watchword for those responsible for engaging in sector ministry, whether a diocesan advisory role or chaplaincy in secular institutions. A dual role post means that the sector interest will be pursued part-time. In many cases half-time is assumed whilst other DRMs have sessions or days each week specified. Questions need to be asked. Is the time allocation sufficient? Perhaps this post was previously full-time—if so, what must be scaled down? In contrast a new sector post may be focused on building up a ministry from scratch with fewer preconceptions. What administrative support is to be available and where? Thought should be given beforehand to where the sector ministry might best be located—at the vicarage, in the diocesan office, in the secular institution or somewhere else. Issues of diocesan geography and convenience, resources and colleague contact are crucial for DRMs who need flexible arrangements in order

---

27 John Finney, *The Well Church Book* (London: Scripture Union/CPAS, 1991) pp 69–94; Robert Warren, *Building Missionary Congregations* (London: Church House Publishing, 1995) pp 47ff.

to be effective. All these matters are, generally speaking, the responsibility of the diocesan board or group where the policy and budget for the sector role is located and to whom the DRM are accountable. The chairperson of the board would be the line manager, providing supervision and support on a regular basis. Where there is a departmental structure of sector colleagues, a head of department might be expected to undertake that role. Chaplains in secular institutions will usually have parallel arrangements spelt out in greater detail in a job description covering accountability, budgeting and conditions of service. None of this need conflict with the diocesan bishop having an appropriate relationship with all whom he licences. The important thing is for the DRM to fit comfortably into his or her organization with clarity of expectation and sources of help to hand.

The Prospective Dual Role Minister

So perhaps you are considering dual role ministry yourself, or are responsible for someone who is. What questions should you be asking? Firstly, details of the sector and parochial dimensions need close inspection along the lines suggested above, as well as the kind of partnership proposed in the job description. The bishop's staff may or may not have got it right, but the key question now is, 'is this DRM right for me?' The answer is a mixture of practical and personal considerations. Do you feel equally called by God to both roles? Is the sector or parish the main pull? Will you need to develop new skills in either or both parts? It has happened that, for example, new DRMs from an urban background have experienced unexpected problems adjusting to their rural parishes when they imagined the only learning curve would be in the sector ministry. Personality type and knowing yourself are important. Myers Briggs Type Indicators and other typologies offer helpful insights into the different approaches to ministry amongst the clergy.[28] There is, however, no single personality blueprint for DRM! Some abilities are God's gift to us while others are skills to be acquired and honed. The challenge of many dual role posts is that they require different temperaments and qualities within one human being whose personality, gifts and skills will probably not match the complete (but idealistic) 'person specification.' Some people thrive on diversity and move easily between different modes of ministry and church life: being/doing, pioneering/consolidating, chaplain/adviser, pastor/prophet, virtuoso/team player. Others can be overwhelmed by this. It is important to realize therefore that being a DRM requires a robust and flexible approach, keeping a sense of proportion and self-worth within the constituent ministries and the entirety of the appointment.

The Job Description

Dual role posts highlight a problem we have in the Church with job descriptions. While sector responsibilities are often well-defined, there is a historic

---

28 Lawrence and Diana Osborn, *God's Diverse People* (London: Darton, Longman & Todd, 1991) pp 98–119.

resistance towards too defined a description of parish ministry. We speak of clergy as office holders rather than employees, paid a stipend rather than a salary, which frees them to minister at their discretion. As the Ordinal makes clear, this is a weighty trust and responsibility, but a parish can collude with this by being vague about its vision and plans. Job descriptions for DRMs would be improved enormously if only a discussion took place prior to appointment, which continued during the key first twelve months, about what the vicar is needed to do in the parish. One PCC discovered that a release from maintenance ministry freed their half-time vicar to engage in a more mission-focused ministry, enlarging the church at its edges. There are signs of a subtle shift from covenant to contractual thinking about ministry, indeed some PCCs have a more robust view of ministry 'value for money' in return for parish share paid. Job descriptions therefore need to hold a balance between economic and pastoral approaches: dual role posts are two jobs and a particular ministry lifestyle. Perhaps an alternative title, for example, 'Ministry Profile' rather than 'Job Description' might help? Certainly the following range of headings should be considered:

1   Job title (carefully agreed and accurately described for both roles)
2   Appointed by, accountable to (eg bishop, diocesan board chair etc)
3   Preamble—what the job description is for
4   Time commitment—the split between roles/responsibilities/day off
5   Residence—parsonage/own home/house for duty/other—clear responsibilities
6   Expected scope of ministry: description including, for example, parish statement or recent mission audit priorities; in the sector role—the predecessor's and board's annual report will help; who has been doing what? in what direction are things moving?
7   Secretarial and administrative support for each role—who, how much, based where? Equipment eg answerphone, fax, computer to be provided—who pays?
8   Sunday and midweek worship commitments in the parish
9   Supervision and support, from whom and how frequently?
10 Training provision for the appointment, in-service training etc paid for by?
11 Finance and expenses—the split between parish and diocese
12 Terms of office—Freehold/Priest-in-Charge? For how long? Is it renewable? Written into one combined licence or two separate licences?
13 Review provision—when, by whom, who can request it?
14 Procedures for resolving difficulties—line manager, discipline etc.
15 Link between licence(s), job description and any contract with the diocese
16 Signatories to the job description, dated

Some believe that job descriptions are of limited value in clerical posts. Certainly it is difficult to capture the implicit activity of the vicar particularly where there is a reluctance to analyse use of time. Dual role posts, however, by virtue of their divergent expectations, force the issue: DRMs want to be wanted, to be available, yet feel frustrated sensing that they have no control over their time. Job descriptions offer an opportunity to take more control and to become pro-active rather than reactive. The bulk of this thinking is best done before licensing and adjustments can be made at review. What are nearly always more troublesome to put right later are misunderstandings due to lack of clarity or negotiation at an earlier stage. The best dual role job descriptions are functionally effective, providing in both roles a sense of direction, and at least in outline a process of future development. A dual role without a job description but with enthusiasm and high expectations will leave the door open to burn-out.

4

Sustaining Dual Role Ministries

Healthy, Whole and Holy

When dual role ministers come together, it can be quite useful to compare diaries because they provide hints as to how we are sustained in ministry. One minister proudly exhibited her neat and colour-coded planning, another was reluctant to interpret his haphazard scribblings, yet another doubted whether any method of organizing oneself actually worked. Dual role posts sharply focus the need for all ministers to keep healthy, whole and holy. It is in trying to maintain wholeness in the face of two competing spheres of ministry that DRMs particularly experience difficulty and stress. These experiences vary enormously amongst DRMs and can change in character over the years. For example, early on in an advisory post it can be unnerving not being quite sure if we are doing enough of what the diocese expects, while five years on we may feel overwhelmed by too much to do. Although, as we have noted, personality is important, it is possible to identify a number of key pieces in the jigsaw without which the picture of a wholesome ministry will remain incomplete—relating to people and structures, time management, skills and resources, spirituality, family and leisure. Morale sinks when insufficient pieces are in place. It may be significant that our prayer life, families and time off are often subjects which overworked DRMs are most coy about. DRM may implicitly exaggerate a 'doing' ministry over a 'being' ministry, and more reflective personalities can find a dominant activism oppressive.

People and Structures

DRMs relate to different people and contexts in different ways—in the parish usually as leader and pastoral carer, in the diocese or secular organization possibly as a team member and specialist voice. We need to know where we are, building up relationships which energize and replenish us, and using frameworks that liberate the ministry task. Some ministers find constantly switching from pastoral to sector mode and back irksome, others will find it stimulating. The concepts of 'contract and covenant' have been used to describe the different natures of these roles. Sector ministry usually works to clear aims and objective with deadlines, and is primarily about 'doing,' while pastoral ministry is more relationally focused, and 'being' is more important. Good communication skills are vital because DRMs need to understand different modes of church life where local church culture, expectations, assumptions and habits of thought are very different from what is normally found on boards and committees. A further difficulty arises when DRMs are expected to demonstrate the 'good practice' of their sector specialism in their own local congregations as an example to others! The opportunity to innovate is not always welcomed in traditional settings and a lay training adviser, for example, might find critical eyes focused on her/his rural parishes where lay ministry may be more difficult to develop. However, the adviser carries credibility when advising clergy struggling with the same problem.

Time Management

Time is for many DRMs the most difficult area to manage. It involves working with different, even competing criteria.[29] It might be possible to leave a diocesan meeting early in order to take a funeral, but it is not possible to do the reverse! Both roles will sometimes expect more than is feasible from the individual and time management is crucial for physical, mental and spiritual health. It is useful to ask whether the job will allow the minister to dedicate a number of days or sessions a week to each role. A three-session day gives a weekly plan of seven sessions in each role and seven off. This might be helpful framework for some, for others an impossibility. It may be that most ministry is more 'messy' and eludes structuring, and that DRM means both roles most days, so checking the balance of time in each role periodically is wise. Planning ahead is probably the key tool for enabling DRM, particularly in anticipating peak times in each role and likely clashes between pieces of work. Distinguishing the important and the urgent pinpoints our priorities. Diarying in adequate preparation time so that important parish events or sector commitments happen without last minute panic is essential. The 'lead time' for a training event might be a year or more, writing a policy paper a month or two, while chaplaincy and parish ministry follow both shorter weekly and seasonal rhythms.

Taking Time Out

DRMs have found it advisable to put generous 'green verges' of unallocated time in their diaries, as a way of catching breath amidst all that has to be done and leaving room for the unexpected. Using a pencil with a rubber in the diary reminds us that things can be changed, while learning ways of saying 'no' or 'not

29 Stephen R Covey and A Roger Merrill, *First Things First* (London: Simon & Schuster, 1994).

yet' can also help DRMs pace themselves. Diarying in regular days off, holidays and recreation, family time, retreats, in-service training opportunities and reading time at an advanced stage prevents essential sources of nourishment being crowded out. Spreading work away from home broadly through the year gives an advisable balance, especially if the parish or our families are prone to complain that the vicar 'is never here.' Advisers who tour dioceses need to manage travelling time safely and be realistic about the number of meetings that can be arranged for one day. Finally we each have in our 'biological clock' a basic time manager—determining when we are at our most creative or energetic and how much rest we need. Above all, DRMs must cherish and protect their time, especially the day off, without guilt. Coping with guilt (imposed externally or from within) is one of the major problems of ordained ministry, particularly where the individual works alone.

Support, Skills and Resources

DRMs often develop a real skill for resourcing themselves! However, certain cornerstones of support are essential, some of which should be explored before licensing and featured in the job description. For both roles a proper induction process is necessary, as is a twelve-month review with the appropriate 'line manager' (eg archdeacon, chair of diocesan board) at which time adjustments can be made. Likewise, supervision on a regular basis, perhaps six-weekly, right from appointment, gives a firm foundation for dual roles. Ministers can develop further support in work consultancy and colleague networks. All these will feed into the diocesan scheme of ministerial appraisal. A key skill to practice is delegation, both in the parish to church officers and members, and in the sector domain to colleagues, volunteers and secretaries. Inadequate administrative support can undermine the effectiveness of DRMs and is a frequent cause for concern, while learning how to best use a desk in the diocesan office is important. DRMs should provide for in-service training in their budget and be in close contact with the CME officer in the diocese. Sector ministries may have their own conferences and training, while excellent courses on 'being an adviser,' 'consultancy skills,' 'moving into rural ministry' and other topics are available in the Church.[30] Giving time to CME is an investment which DRMs ignore at their peril. Most DRMs have not ministered this way before so assistance with the transitions and the new skills necessary to succeed is essential; being priest-in-charge of villages is different from being a suburban team vicar, and being diocesan Social Responsibility Officer is not the same as running a local community project. The national Network for Dual Role Ministry aims to support DRMs and may be particularly helpful in the early stages of an appointment.[31]

---

30 An annual national training programme is arranged by the Board of Education in London; rural induction is provided by the National Rural Officer at the National Agricultural Centre, Warwickshire.
31 Contact: Nigel Peyton, Dunham House, Westgate, Southwell, Notts NG25 0JL. Telephone: (01636) 814331. Fax: (01636) 815084. E-mail: SDBF@John316.com

Spirituality

There may not be a distinctive spirituality for dual role ministers, but making the time to develop it is obviously important, especially for those working in a less conventional field of ministry. A spiritual director can help us establish a pattern of prayer or to explore new possibilities—DRMs often need to adjust their spiritual nurture to suit new circumstances. Parish-based DRMs may find support in worshipping with their communities; others may feel oppressed by their liturgical week or not have one at all. Being part of a housegroup, praying regularly with clerical neighbours or sector colleagues have all been found valuable. Regular quiet times with God and periodic retreats and pilgrimage, our reading and leisure pursuits all contribute to our holiness and well-being.

Stress

The need to manage stress is an important part of the minister's survival skills. It appears Dual Role always ends up more than two halves (0.5+0.5=1.5!), even when the foregoing advice has been accepted. It is actually when things are going well that the danger of overwork lurks. Demands will probably increase on both fronts over time as people get to know the minister and it is important to build in adequate space for reflection, especially during the first year. DRMs must be encouraged to look after themselves, and the sanctity of the day off is something to be established early, in the mind of the minister as well as of others in sector or parish. It is important for ministry, personal health and happiness. The image of the juggler comes to mind. It is fun being so busy to begin with, but soon we cannot keep up, as extra pieces of ministry tumble into our overstretched schedule. DRM stress usually focuses on losing control of the constituent parts of our ministry and the disintegration of the whole picture. Occupational psychologists pinpoint the lack of control amidst a sea of fast-moving change as the most significant factor in experiencing stress today.[32] Rushing things 'just in time' is stressful, but so also is not knowing where to start in some aspect of our ministry, or indeed, questioning the very purpose of it all. The feeling that we are not delivering what God, the bishop or parishioners expect, less still, what we expect of ourselves, can seriously undermine our confidence. We go to bed at night worrying about all we have not done today and all we have to do tomorrow. We need to understand the causes, symptoms and consequences of the stress we experience in dual role. Wanda Nash reminds us that wholeness means caring for all of ourselves, body, mind and spirit. She offers helpful stress skills, insights into our behaviour mechanisms and simple exercises which free us from the tyranny of demands. Her sharp challenge to those who feel they have too many demands is, honestly, how much of this 'over' demand comes out of my choice? From

---

32 Cary Cooper, interviewed in the *Independent*, 6 January 1998 p 15.

pride and ineffective relationships or work patterns perhaps? The more demands there are the more we must take charge of ourselves and be recharged. We must let up to avoid being laid up.[33]

Dual Role in Difficulties

While many dual role posts are problematic and challenging, a few end in disaster. Failure is not always the minister's fault—some roles will never partner well, others are impossibly demanding or under-resourced and we should not establish posts which damage people. However, undisclosed inner motives may be significant. Some ministers' hearts are really set on a full-time role in one half of their post, so the other suffers; some want to escape parish ministry, while others simply become lost between both roles. Dual role ministers may discover that the church tradition and theology of mission in which they were schooled are in conflict with other views of church and community implicit in their jobs. A lack of grip on the gospel faith, an unprofessional ministry lifestyle, poor spiritual resources or family problems may also contribute to breakdown. These indicators suggest that when dual role is not 'first choice' it is unlikely to be the best choice. The reason for failure may alert church leaders to the reasons why dual role posts can be difficult to fill in the first place. Paradoxically such posts may attract both the most able clergy and the weakest, yet satisfying neither. While not bringing out the best in the capable ministers, dual role may harm those already carrying personal difficulties. Careful supervision during the first year will reveal early signs of problems and senior leaders should not allow DRMs to soldier on when a pastoral conclusion to an unsustainable ministry is more appropriate.

---

33 Wanda Nash, *At Ease With Stress* (London: Darton, Longman & Todd, 1988) pp 31, 43, 46–54, 184–192. See also her Grove Pastoral booklet P 42 *Living with God at the Vicarage.*

5
A Theology for Role Complexity in Ministry

First Choice

The arrangement of Jesus' parables in St Matthew's gospel emphasizes choice. The saying about serving two masters has become a commonplace for the pitfalls of divided loyalties: 'No one can serve two masters; for a slave will either hate the one and love the other, or be devoted to the one and despise the other. You cannot serve God and wealth' (Matt 6.24 NRSV). Jeremias notes that many slaves did serve two masters, especially when brothers left an estate undivided after their father's death,[34] while the 'Gospel of Thomas' gives the saying a more practical edge, 'Jesus said, "A man cannot mount two horses; he cannot stretch two bows. A servant cannot serve two masters; either he will honour the one and the other he will scorn."'[35] This parable is about choosing an undistracted faith. Throughout his ministry, Jesus was challenged by different loyalties—the crowds, his disciples, the Jewish Law, Caesar and God. It is in an incarnational theology that dual role ministry finds blessing and focus amidst complexity. Not only did Jesus steadfastly do the will of the Father, a strong theme in the fourth gospel, but in his very being as human and divine he held together the loyalties of earth and heaven. Pannenberg reminds us that human nature is ordained for the incarnation of the eternal Son in it; though we ourselves cannot fulfil this destiny of ours in our own finite strength, we share in the ministry of Jesus, God's first chosen.[36] Jesus' authority and clarity of purpose (witnessed particularly in the Passion) points to a deep-rooted spirituality which could sustain all the competing demands made daily upon him. Jesus' ministry contains plenty of good practice for DRMs; note for example how Jesus copes with the urgent, prioritizes and prays.

Incarnation and Improvisation

Incarnational theology keeps all ministry firmly on the ground and Christ-centred (Ephesians 4.1–16). DRMs serve one Master in two ways. The glory of dual roles is that, thus grounded, ministers can cross boundaries, make connections and create partnerships in new ways. An adviser's apostolic role in the wider Church as lay educator or evangelist, frees her parish from local narrowness while reminding her of reality; the chaplain in the hospital or educational establishment proclaims God in the secular world but equally feeds his parish with the particular needs and opportunities of 'God on Monday.' The Church's mission is therefore well served by DRMs whose divergent responsibilities break the minis-

---

34 Joachim Jeremias, *The Parables of Jesus* (London: SCM, 1972) p 192f.
35 'The Coptic Gospel of Thomas' 47 in David R Cartlidge and David L Dungan, *Documents for the Study of the Gospels* (London: Collins, 1980) p 30.
36 Wolfhart Pannenberg, *Systematic Theology Volume 2* (Edinburgh: T & T Clark, 1994) p 385f.

try mould. The bridge-building possibilities are exciting, but in as much as dual role brings out ministry treasure, new and old, it may also have a more radical destabilizing effect on 'the way we do thing here.' As we noted in the opening section, there is an unresolved struggle going on in the Church to find order amidst new diversity in ministry patterns, and to redefine the clerical role.[37]

It may be that the Church is on the edge of what historians and future-watchers call a paradigm shift—the painful change from one world view to another, for example, towards mission without buildings or ministry without clergy. This mirrors a wider concern about complex modern social institutions and our roles within them, and it may be that DRM is rather well placed to explore this.[38] It is both a symptom of and response to uncertainty in a Church in decline and its character is one of improvisation. It is significant that a distinguished social scientist writing about re-engineering postmodern organizations, and a renowned bishop reflecting on the provisionality which characterizes all human existence, each use the same image—that of the jazz band and the jazz player. The genius of jazz is improvisation: 'if we can find the courage to abandon the text when necessary and improvise in response to the audience and its dialogue with us, we soon learn that we are making a new kind of music with people rather than forcing them to listen to the few tunes we have in our repertoire.'[39] Perhaps it was this very quality which distinguished the ministry of the incarnate Son of God? There is a great deal of first rate 'first choice' dual role ministry around in the Church. We are blessed with some extremely creative improvisers who can collaborate with others. Collaboration has been a ministry buzz-word recently but its interpretation has sometimes been a rather unproductive organizational or interpersonal clustering. The jazz band, however, recognizes every player as a potential soloist while never losing its corporate rhythm. DRMs capture this spirit and, as the business world says, should be given the necessary 'headroom' and support to deliver the goods. The Church is, above all, a vocational organization where a great deal of ministry needs to be undertaken by motivated, self-starting ministers. DRMs in particular need sufficient energy to head off in two directions at the same time, and (to continue jazz imagery) will have the ability to solo on two instruments!

Exciting Ministers

Much of this booklet has been concerned with the practicalities of dual role ministry and how to maximize its blessings. The vast majority of DRMs enjoy their varied work and are appreciated for all they do; they give 'added value.' It appears that dual role is an ideal choice for some ministers at the right period in their ministry, as well as suiting the pastoral arrangements required in the Church. In a forthcoming study about what happens to clergy in the first years of ministry

37 Advisory Board of Ministry, *Order in Diversity* (London: ABM, 1993).
38 Jonathan Sacks, *The Politics of Hope* (London: Jonathan Cape, 1997) p 235f.
39 Richard Holloway, *Dancing on the Edge* (London: Harper Collins, 1997) p 167; Peter F Drucker, *Post Capitalist Society* (Oxford: Butterworth—Heinemann, 1993) p 84.

it seems that early diversification by some ministers may lead to a dual role appointment at a later stage.[40] There is some anecdotal evidence that for most people, one dual role ministry is enough, though a few have enjoyed serial dual roles! Further research into the long-term effects of dual role posts is needed to gauge this. Our discussion here about dual role ministry also touches other pressing questions about non-stipendiary ministry, local ministry teams and part-time ministry. A recent essay revisiting the neglected area of ministry in secular employment echoes what we have said about dual roles: 'Nobody has ever said that being an MSE is meant to be easy, but its very difficulty means that it offers enormous scope for richness and wholeness.'[41]

Hard places to be can often be visionary places and many DRMs express a refreshing excitement about their ministries. This is encouraging because DRM highlights rather well the priestly qualities sought after by the Church of England in the selection criteria: it holds local *pastoral* ministry together with wider *apostolic* responsibilities; it needs secure *spiritual* roots in order to prioritize *missionary* opportunities; it needs *theological* reflection, a *prophetic* cutting edge and an effective *collaborative* leadership style. In all, DRMs need to be self aware, that is to say, robust and comfortable in themselves and in ministerial role, intellectually able to work under pressure within a changing climate.[42] A practical theology for dual roles is therefore strongly incarnational in its challenge to realize the kingdom in today's ministry. An incarnational theology gives significance amidst the ambiguities and complexities of roles in ministry. As in Christ the old and new covenants meet, so in dual roles the minister improvises with treasure new and old, with skill and integrity in the constituent parts and entirety of his or her appointment. When the experience along the way is mixed this does not diminish the choice, for as the poet observes, 'Priests have a long way to go.'[43] If Dual Role Ministry is to be a preferred choice then the Church will surely benefit from understanding it better.

40 Neil Burgess, *Putting Out into Deep Waters* (Bury St Edmunds: Kevin Mayhew, 1998).
41 Antony Hurst, *Theology of Ministry in Secular Employment* (London: Diocese of Southwark, 1997) p 37f.
42 Advisory Board of Ministry, *Going to a Selection Conference* (London: ABM, 1996) pp 9–11.
43 R S Thomas 'The Priest' in *Collected Poems 1945-1996* (London: Dent, 1993) p 196.